Warrior Yogi Mindset

Not only to Life...; How to give a response, not a reaction..

Dinesh Talekar (Dhivo)

ISBN: 978-93-343-6150-6

Publisher: D Innovation Media | Dhivo | Dinesh Dilip Vijaya Talekar

Dhivo.in | DhivoYoga@gmail.com | +91 7040038881

Price: INR 300

1st Edition 21st July 2025

(My Mother's Birthday – Vijaya Dilip Talekar)

Index:

"Even animals feel deeply for their own,
But if your heart awakens with compassion for others too,
Then know this — humanity is still alive within you." — Dhivo

--

At every place, the mind
craves to become "stable and settled"…
It seeks a comfort zone or
some form of support —
just to run away
from uncertainty and insecurity.

— Dhivo

--

Many people…
not only can't tolerate others' goodness,
but at times, they can't even stand
the success or virtues of their own people.

And sadly, this reaction often
comes naturally to them —
so unconsciously, that they themselves
fail to notice it.

No matter how sincerely
you act or do good,
they'll always find a way
to pick flaws in something.

They may praise you,
but just as they're about to leave,
they'll slip in a grain of salt... — Dhivo

--

Don't Quit:

A truly capable person becomes like a versatile bird — one who, while fulfilling responsibilities, dives deep into the ocean's depths, then rises to soar through the skies, walks and runs on land, falls, gets up again, and with renewed strength, keeps carrying the burden of duty on his shoulders — tirelessly playing the great game of life and family. - Dhivo

--

The Charioteer:

Writer: Dhivo (Dinesh Dilip Talekar)

Who has seen tomorrow, my friend? Anyway, who waits around till old age? Let's live today, while we still can...

The future—well, life itself teaches us how to deal with that when it comes, doesn't it?

And even then, the vehicle must cooperate too, right?

I've got just one vehicle of my own.

But I have a few rare friends—those who, even in the dead of night, pick up the phone,

and without a second thought, hand me the keys to any of their vehicles.

Once, I took a friend's car in Rishikesh and suddenly set off toward Devprayag.

That journey brought me into the silent company of many sacred lands of meditation and penance.

I spent three full days wandering through Uttarakhand—alone—

through Mussoorie, Dehradun, Haridwar, and eventually came back to Tapovan, near Laxman Jhula.

The experience was what they call an "eye-opener."

It felt like life revealed something deeply transforming.

Vehicles will always be available.

But what truly matters is the intensity of the charioteer's will to live.

The friends I mentioned—they've boiled life down to its essence,

and in this temporary life, they've tasted even the smallest petal of what's eternal.

You see, this isn't really about vehicles.

It's about the expansion of the soul.

And when we do talk about vehicles,

I must say—like I said earlier—

I have only one vehicle that I can truly call my own.

And there's no other vehicle that compares to it.

No matter how many times someone asks,

I cannot hand this one over—

not until the right time comes.

This vehicle has been with me since birth.

Its uniqueness is such that I could spend an entire lifetime describing it.

Yet even then, I couldn't truly say it "belongs" to me.

Still, there has to be a certain ownership—

an acceptance of stewardship,

as long as that ownership is rooted in humanity and friendship.

And yes, this vehicle is still running.

It walks with me, moment by moment.

It's because of it that I'm able to move about this world—

sometimes with abandon,

sometimes with caution.

In light or in darkness,

to travel alone, to meet friends, family, or even strangers—

I must always journey using this same chariot.

And this miraculous chariot allows me to meet others too—fully, deeply.

What's astonishing is how it subtly changes every day—

how it feels slightly different each morning.

And every 7 to 10 years, it goes to two master engineers— "Mr. Conscious" and "Mr. Subconscious"— and returns fully modified.

Now you might say,

"Hey Dinesh Talekar, what is this amazing vehicle you're going on about?"

And I would reply—

"It's not just mine—each of you has one too.

Every one of you possesses one such vehicle.

And each is unique, irreplaceable, and divine in its own way."

That vehicle… that chariot...

is what we call the body.

There are many other vehicles in the world,

but instead of chasing them and getting entangled in worldly complications,

why not stay engaged—at least temporarily—in the chariot nature gifted us? Let's anchor the soul in it—

so we may stay truly alive, and live a life of complete, human experience.

Through this chariot, may we form true connections— with all, or at least with a few chosen souls.

Only then will the journey of this chariot and its charioteer become truly meaningful.

...Aligning humane frequencies with the contemporary souls of quantum friendship... — Dhivo (Dinesh Talekar)

--

"Timely" Beings...

Writer: Dhivo (Dinesh Dilip Talekar)

Dhivo – One who is on the path of understanding…

Has the circus of life already begun for you?

Two kinds of people exist:

—Those who don't know what to do with the time they have...

—And those who never get the time at all.

And some?

They don't even realize that they're supposed to live this ticking moment of life.

Why?

Because either they're counting the minutes of existence...

Or just killing time, scrolling, strolling, or surviving...

But this priceless time—

It's meant to be lived fully, humanely, consciously.

Not simply "passed."

The wise village elders used to say,

"Even animals live for themselves... even a dog fills its belly..."

So the question remains—

What are we supposed to do with this time?

Should we chase wealth and property?

Or just enjoy ourselves until we burn out?

Or keep dragging on this same tired routine—

Either with complaints...

Or with the hollow indulgence that pretends to be contentment?

If you say, “I don’t really know...”

Well, not knowing is the first step towards truly living.

If something makes sense to you, do share—

Because sharing is caring, right?

Sometimes we spend our time like diamonds...

Sometimes like cheap lentils...

But both have their own place in the moment.

Sometimes you must deposit time into your wisdom account,

And sometimes you must taste the bitter experiences of time

with honey-dipped fingers.

But amid all of this—

what matters most is to stay aware and present,

so that we can lose ourselves once more

in the dance of living. - Dhivo

Let's speak of awakening, of living—

Because once we die, people will speak about us anyway—

for 13 or 14 days at least.

Though, admittedly, they talk a little more

on the first and the tenth day.

When I step into the marketplace of society

and observe people closely,

I often wonder—

Am I the one getting it wrong?

Because most people carry on

as if this day will never end—

let alone life itself.

Some are deeply burdened.

Some are endlessly entertained.

Some are always struggling.

Some are too busy enjoying to ever reflect.

“Let it go on as it is”

—This is the default setting of our mind.

And even those who seem to be doing something “different”

often appear to be further tightening

the chains of worldly entanglement.

Honestly, there's nothing wrong with either of these views.

But in both,

our true questions—

about life, self, and meaning—

get pushed aside.

Instead, our daily tools for survival

eat away at our precious time—

like termites in diamonds.

And maybe, just maybe—

true life, authentic living, gets left behind.

This thought haunts me

when I watch my own time slipping away—

and see others' time vanish too—

while standing in the crowd of life.

At times, when I reflect on time— deep within the folds of memory and consciousness— in the chambers of heartbeats, emotions, and awakened or dormant awareness, I feel a choking lump in my throat.

A whirlpool pulls at my navel— a storm of silent anxiety.

They say,

"A wise one learns from the stumble of another…"

But how often do we really practice this?

And who said we must only turn to spirituality?

That too must arise organically.

The path of karma—of action—is inevitable.

Even a little experience teaches this truth.

But each of us must define what karma truly means for us.

Think of Krishna, the Buddha, Mahavira...

Sant Dnyaneshwar, Ramakrishna Paramhansa, Tukaram...

And later, Shivaji Maharaj, Mahatma Phule, Dr. Babasaheb Ambedkar—

did their lives not know hardship and stumbles?

But we never get the time

to contemplate their lives—

to understand, absorb, or practice what they stood for.

And so the same cycle rises again—

The same battlefield of confusion.

We don't know what to do with our time,

nor how to get time in the first place.

But perhaps— if one becomes aware and awake, then even "understanding time" becomes possible.

To understand life, you must enter its sanctum...

And maybe—just maybe— that moment of true living will arrive.

But by then, the opportunity to truly live it

might already be gone. Time waits for no one. And once it's gone— it's really gone. That's the one thing about time that's always perfectly clear.

: Dhivo (Dinesh Dilip Talekar)

#Dhivo #RebelliousThinking #TimeMatters #ConsciousLife #WarriorYogi #SpiritualHumanism #BoilingBlood #LifeReflections

--

"Who is true, and who is false—
that must be answered by peering into one's own inner conscience.

But if real, genuine humans don't learn to forgive, to absorb the hurt, to overlook the wrongs, then survival itself becomes difficult.

Because at every step, you'll keep encountering the cunning, the selfish, the betrayers— People who exploit you, manipulate opportunities, steal credit, and show no gratitude— hearts turned inside out with crooked intent.

And when faced with such toxic behaviour, the breath of a true-hearted person may begin to suffocate... – Dhivo

--

Boiling blood - a wakeup call from within..

Rebel against corrupt politicians:

"Prostitute, beggar, eunuch, and animal" — these words have been wrongly imposed upon the innocent and the voiceless.
The ones who truly deserve these labels are some of today's shameless and deceptive politicians.

A handful of fraudsters have reduced the nation to dust and ashes.
But let's not dishonour even those words — for using them for such corrupt demons would be an insult to the words themselves.
Yes, they have sunk that low...
In truth, these four words aren't insults at all — they feel more like the four unseen pillars of humanity.
Because when we look at the so-called four pillars of our democracy today,
It seems they are infested — with rot, termites, and disease.

Maybe you won't fully understand what I'm trying to say.
Because this demon of unrighteousness — this Evil Giant "Bhasmasur" — has spread so wildly, that no words can truly capture its horror.

And so, I can only bow to Mother India — with a gaze full of sorrow and pain…

— Dinesh Talekar (Dhivo)

--

"There was once the fire of Shivaji Maharaj in our blood…
But now, by gathering in wrong alliances, we've ended up becoming Aurangzeb ourselves…
Oh! Have some shame!
It's still not too late — turn back before it's completely lost." : Dhivo

--

Sarcastic Friendly Love:

Why should we even praise your wealth?
You neither understand friendship nor humanity.
All you do is chew at the bones of selfishness.
Never in life have I seen someone as self-centered as you.
All you care about is eating, drinking, and lying around like a bull.
And then you sit back, nurturing your bulging belly, fat, and eventually, diseases.

It's shameful to even call people like you a 'friend'—or even a 'human.'
How do you not understand anything?

But never give up on life, my friend…

Let the sky collapse,
Or let sorrow as huge as a mountain strike—
But never, ever stop loving life with all your heart, my friend. Never give up on living, my friend… : Dhivo

--

A life untouched by failure is an incomplete life...
Because true, unshakable success is earned only after facing failure. — Dhivo

--

"Sangham Sharanam Gachchhami"

(I take refuge in the community) : Dhivo

How thick-skinned can a herd be?
Except for a few individuals, the rest are just a crowd.
Should we pickle your awards and honors now?

We are proud of you—
That you've received Padma Shri, Padma Bhushan, The Arjuna Award, Khel Ratna,
Or the Filmfare Lifetime Achievement Award.

But these awards aren't just meant to be flaunted on your chest.
And receiving them doesn't mean your journey or mission is complete.
In fact, the greater the award, the greater the responsibility that comes with it.

Seeing your awards, fame, and wealth—
We wonder how enormous your responsibility must truly be!
What use are all these achievements if you don't use them
For the welfare of society, the nation, or the world?

Look around— So many overwhelming problems stare us in the face,
And yet you're not even willing to speak about them?

All you can manage is a two-line tweet—
To express sorrow or offer condolence.
Beyond that, you are silent.

Oh intellectuals stripped of humanity,
Do you even realize the moral duty That rests upon your towering shoulders? And here you are… tweeting and commenting?

When Dr. Ambedkar said, "Educate, Organize, and Agitate," Did he say it only for Dalits?

But no… We prefer just chanting,
"Sangham Sharanam Gachchhami"
And continue living our isolated, pleasure-seeking lives.

You have reached the highest peaks—
Now, you owe something to humanity.

So why not come together—
You, and others of similar vision and influence—
And form a strong collective?

Why not make an effort to face and solve
The crises humanity, nature, and the world are going through?

You may be sportspersons, film stars, or leading industrialists— Then unite. Form a team. Show us your leadership and management skills.

Build a strong, golden "Think Tank."
Use it to hold governments accountable And channel real, people-centric work. Call upon legal minds, social reformers, scientists — Come together—create a fusion! Build a powerful organization That can give voice to burning issues.

But no—
You just want to live for yourself,
For your family, your awards, your fame, your wealth.

You've chosen this hypnotic, selfish life for yourself, haven't you?

If we—these passionate, young, inspired minds—
Were in your position, We would have risked everything—fame and awards alike— For the welfare of humanity.

You've reached such heights—
Can't you build a bridge of eternal friendship between nations?

Can't you inspire today's youth toward creativity, innovation, and meaningful living?
Can't you sow seeds of morality and humanity in society?
My beloved icons, noble personalities—
With folded hands, I sincerely plead with you:
You have the power to solve thousands of critical problems. You can lay the foundation for countless great initiatives.
Just take one step toward the Golden Age… Form a community of strong, like-minded souls.
Throw just one stone toward the sky—
And watch…
Even the sky will begin to crack open,
And from it will rain the sacred river of evolved humanity. —: Dhivo

--

Failure isn't just the first step to success — it's the ninety-ninth one too...
Because water doesn't boil at 99, it boils at 100 degrees. : - Dhivo

--

— A Blazing Cry from the Conscience of the Great Souls:

Dr. Narendra Dabholkar was shot down—
So what difference does it make to you?
You're the walking dead.
But he was a living human being.

He wasn't your relative, nor of your caste, creed, or blood—
So your response is:
"He died? Well, it wasn't our blood."

Of course.
How could the revolutionary, explosive blood of Gandhi, Bhagat Singh, or Dabholkar ever flow through your veins?

You've been living like soulless corpses for thousands of years.

If someone's asleep, they can be awakened.
But how can we wake you—

When your slumber is not ignorance, but a well-practiced performance?

When someone in your own family dies,
You cry for five or ten days and then settle down.
But if a stranger dies right at your doorstep—
You simply drag their corpse aside
And carry on with your 9-to-5 routine.

And your "so-called ministers and bureaucrats"—
Don't they feel even an ounce of shame?
Even a rhino's hide is not this thick.

A chameleon only changes the color of its skin—
But these vultures are set on turning the whole world pitch black.

Those who silence the voice of truth with bullets
Are nothing but brainwashed human robots.
They have no mind, no soul.
But the real monsters are the white-collared conspirators—
Who are rising to uproot the very foundation of humanity.

So if you still don't wake up
From your ages-old darkness,
Your destruction is inevitable.

Today, you're playing the role of mute spectators—

A drama of cowardice.
But what will you do tomorrow
If your own children are born
Carrying the same explosive spirit of truth and rebellion?

What will you tell them?

"That we let Dabholkar be murdered"?
"That many among us were his ideological opponents,
And instead of fighting him with reason and debate,
We killed him with cowardly violence"?

What will you say?
"That you are not truly our children,
Because our blood was impotent—
And your blood, burning with the fire of revolution, Must have come from somewhere else"?

Will they even want to call you their parents?

Wake up, friends! This is not just a cry—
It's the burning anguish from the conscience of the great ones.
Rise with awakened thought,
Rise with courage,
Rise, my friends—wake up!

— Boiling Blood, - : Dhivo

--

Friends, if you truly wish to achieve meaningful success, then remember the mantra of triumph is — "Burning Passion, Deep Reflection, and Courageous Action." : Dhivo

--

A Whiplash of Satirical Truth:

This morning, during a conversation, a friend remarked:
"Friend, how much sorrow, selfishness, heartlessness, and mental perversion has grown in human life..."

I smiled and replied:
"If mirrors were alive, then after witnessing such terrifying faces of humans every day—millions of them would've committed mass suicide by now!"
— Dhivo

--

Thugs mocking others' pain are found at every street corner...

But it takes a real heart to smile through your own sorrow. — Dhivo

--

Rather than digging up the dead corpses of the past,
it's far better to stand tall in the present and plant the flag of your actions for the future. - Dhivo

--

There is so much to learn in this world… but before you learn everything else, first — learn these:

1. Learn to make mistakes.
2. Learn to stand alone against the tide.
3. Learn to walk into darkness.
4. Learn to raise your voice against injustice.
5. Learn to express your opinion boldly.
6. Learn to say "No."
7. Learn to ask questions.
8. Learn to help and to serve.
9. Learn to love.
10. Learn to be silent.
11. Learn to live in solitude.
12. Learn to travel.
13. Learn to speak to yourself.
14. Learn to think of others.
15. Learn to struggle.

16. Learn to rise above pleasure and pain.
17. Learn to take responsibility and fulfill it.
18. Learn to believe deeply in yourself.
19. Learn for a man to value a woman, and a woman to value a man.
20. Learn to connect with nature.
21. Learn to maintain balanced food, exercise, and sleep.
22. Learn to meditate.
23. Learn to think the highest thoughts.
24. Learn to study.
25. Learn to speak, lead, and act.
26. Learn to dream big.
27. Learn to imagine and create.
28. Learn to live in the present and enjoy life.
29. And above all — learn to live as a true Human Being.
30. And if there's life beyond physical death — learn to seek that too. - Dhivo

--

We consider it our responsibility that every individual of the YuvaShakti Nirman Kendra must master
oratory, leadership, and purposeful action — to establish their own identity.

— Dhivo (Dinesh Talekar)
YuvaShakti Nirman Kendra

--

Try to live like a zero — and you will see, even the richness of the Earth
will begin to flow through you. — Dhivo

--

Love with a heart like a mother's —
learn to embrace others with compassion.
Live with a will like a father's —
be disciplined, and extend a guiding hand to others. — Dhivo

--

All we have to do is sow the 'seed' and initiate the beginning —
Existence itself nurtures it into a mighty tree. — Dhivo

--

In the eyes of a rare few — those awakened to youthful vitality in old age, yet fighting the finality of physical death —
one can see a deep question standing before them:
"We awakened too late… but when will the younger generation receive an education that truly

awakens their inner youthfulness — a life-vision that transforms?
And when will such educators emerge — who ignite youthful awakening and instill humane life-values?"
— Dhivo (Dinesh Talekar)

--

Our education system only tests memory, while all the other priceless human qualities within the youth silently fade away in the process.
And what finally emerges is a so-called "intelligent generation" —
imaginative-less and devoid of humane virtues — proudly carried on your shoulders. — Dhivo

--

We're not saying you should go beyond the law — but at least ensure that humanity does not fall in the eyes of the one standing before you. — Dhivo

--

Nearly 90% of a youth's time is wasted in mocking others and indulging in useless chatter — and in the process, a life more precious than diamonds and rubies slips right through their hands… — Dhivo

--

You waste your entire life in meaningless time-pass, and even in old age, you still crave entertainment.
Keep pampering your body and mind with indulgences —
but remember, to embark upon the Great Journey, one must prove worthy of it.
— Dhivo

--

Rather than having a herd of hundreds of so-called friends,
it's far better to have a small circle of seven or eight virtuous and selfless companions. Or even just one or two — but those who would give their very life for you... Like Krishna and Arjuna, or Krishna and Sudama. — Dhivo

--

If you wish to preserve that hypocritical seriousness
like some of your so-called politicians, bureaucrats, officers, managers, or professors —
then instead of saying “Don’t laugh,”
why not simply point toward the animals directly?
— Dhivo

--

Because of your hypocritical seriousness and so-called professionalism,
human beings have either stopped laughing altogether
or have turned into herds of distorted, hollow laughers…
— Dhivo
--

When we take up a mission or task, starting it is in our hands…
But if we don't know where to stop, the entire game can turn against us. — Dhivo

--

Some people are simply of limited intellect — they don't know when to speak, what to say, or how to behave…
That's still understandable.
But some are of a small heart — they can't even love themselves properly, so what love can they possibly offer others?
— Dhivo
--

We've lost all awareness of what we say and how we behave...
After falling to such depths, how can we even dare to call ourselves human?
Come on — feel some shame.
I'm telling you truly:
Hold your own ears in regret, and now... finally stand on your own feet. — Dhivo

--

"**The true and timeless treasure of Swarajya** lies in
the visionary life and ever-evolving thoughts of Chhatrapati Shivaji Maharaj."
— Dhivo
--

"In the name of serving the poor and the underprivileged,
you are actually nurturing a servant class meant to serve the elite and the wealthy.
From my perspective, this is neither social service nor true charity." — Dhivo

--

"Only that can be called true Vikaas (Development)
which arises from thoughtful action — born of an awakened intellect and a sensitive heart — leading to meaningful work and holistic prosperity, and through that prosperity, brings fulfilment, well-being, and joy into the lives of individuals, society, and all beings." — Dhivo
--

"True social service lies not just in temporarily fulfilling the basic needs of the poor and the needy, but in also providing them with sustainable means of livelihood.
And beyond that, enabling a timeless flow of life through the inner light of meditation, wisdom, devotion, and love."
— Dhivo
--

॥ Igniting the Spark of Consciousness ॥

— Dhivo (Dinesh Talekar)

Let the spark of inspiration sizzle in every breath,

Let a blazing fire of uprising roar in your chest,

Let every nerve pulse with a thirst for victory, Let flames of rebellion ignite in every cell of your mind! Awaken, my friend — it's already too late…

You are lost in a deep unconscious slumber,
Drowned in the darkness of delusion.

Ages have passed, yet your sleep remains unbroken,

The chains of inertia and ignorance still bind your soul.

But now — Rise! Rise with radiant vigor to pierce this darkness,

Join the battle of truth with your full might and presence.

There is no substitute for Sādhanā (spiritual discipline),

Yet carry Sattva — the light of purity — within you.

Seek the path of eternal action through righteous living,

Shatter the illusions of ego, jealousy, envy, lust, greed, and anger.

Love, compassion, and non-violence are radiant paths too,

So are renunciation, devotion, and selfless surrender.

But so are rebellion, war, and fierce resistance — when needed.

So rise — with strength, with blazing inspiration!

Either discover your path, or create it anew…

And ignite again the divine spark of your awakened consciousness.

Let there be a thunderous call, a bold invocation,

A soul-awakening roar of that eternal greatness —
That spark… of luminous, blazing consciousness. - Dhivo

--

Outside a temple of humanity, a sign was displayed — "You may bring in your slippers and shoes, but please leave your ego outside the door before entering."
— Dhivo
--

The corruption of intellect and the transformation of a human into a demonic beast was once shown to mankind through the deeds of Hitler and Ravana.

Yet, even today, nations across the world are foolishly competing
to develop nuclear, chemical, and biological weapons.

But remember—
The next Ravana or Hitler that rises may be the last one…

For the spark of the third world war ignited by such a cruel mind
will inevitably lead to the complete destruction of the Earth. — Dhivo

--

The power of the ego hidden within you is so immense that even your devotion or spiritual practice may turn impotent before it.
A terrifying example of this is Ravana,
whose utter destruction was caused solely by his own ego. — Dhivo

--

But if you truly look deeper, there are only two real enemies —
Ego and Selfishness. — Dhivo

--

Every person who enters our life carries deep significance. Because at times, we may deceive ourselves— but the force that orchestrates our life's journey—
that Nature or that higher Existence—never deceives us.

So, for the divine purpose that Existence has chosen me,
and for everyone who became part of my journey to shape me for that purpose—
I offer my deepest gratitude. — Dhivo
--

Please do not misunderstand what I'm saying.
I am not here to create conflict—
I speak not for argument, but for transformation through meaningful dialogue.
And let me be clear: when necessary,
I will not step back from rebellious action through conscious deeds.
Because what many of you call "social service" today,

reeks of selfish intentions.
What you claim as social work
is, in fact, nothing more than a game of entertainment.

Organizing cultural events,
hosting film-inspired dance and music shows,
glittering award functions,
political speeches and competitive gatherings,
or even arranging free trips to religious places—
Don't pamper the ego in the name of social service.

And if entertainment is your chosen medium of social work,
then at least dedicate it to those most deprived:
construction workers, sugarcane cutters,
and the labouring class with no access to any leisure.

Because when entertainment is absent—
and when self-declared social workers like you ignore them—
these neglected people find their only remaining form of "entertainment" in unconscious sexual indulgence.

And what results?
A dangerously surging population—growing faster than a bullet train.
You can already see the consequences.

— Dhivo

--

Sometimes, it feels like all painters might be profound… but how come none of them seem truly mature?

Why has not even a single artist ever felt like painting the great souls or divine deities with a pure, heartfelt smile?

Almost all paintings depict them with serious expressions.
And it's not possible that they never smiled…

At such moments, I feel envious of Japan and China—
just look at their Laughing Buddha!
— Dhivo

--

"From the very moment we arrive on this Earth, the wheel of karma is already in motion — karma is inevitable.
Forgive me, but either you choose meditation or business — what truly matters is your conscious choice towards the highest awareness and a vision rooted in the highest values." — Dhivo

--

"If a region is underdeveloped, we can understand it — and with a shower of developmental efforts, that region can be nurtured into progress. But when a person or a group, already blessed with economic prosperity, still carries a backward and narrow mindset, then witnessing such intellectual poverty truly evokes deep pity." — Dhivo

--

"Foresight, determination, and courage are essential —

but unless one takes a leap into the darkness, struggles, and works hard in reality, the rays of true progress will never be seen." — Dhivo

--

Anti-Beggary Law?
Is Giving Alms to Beggars Right or Wrong?

Answer:

It's neither entirely wrong nor completely right.
What truly matters is maintaining a balanced and thoughtful approach between the two.
To decide who deserves alms and who doesn't, one must awaken their conscience, guided by discernment (vivek) and compassion.

Once this awareness arises, the debate itself becomes irrelevant.
The argument — whether giving alms is wrong or whether it is a noble social service — simply doesn't arise.

Who begs?
There are generally two kinds of people who seek alms:

Those whose physical, mental, and spiritual energies are severely depleted, and

Those whose energies are established at the highest spiritual peaks, or are on the path toward such elevation.

For example — Gautam Buddha, Mahatma Gandhi, Sant Dnyaneshwar, and many great saints — all sustained themselves through alms.

There is not just a semantic difference but a difference in purpose between the alms given to saints and the begging of ordinary beggars.
Some beg out of laziness and tamasic inertia, while others are genuinely compelled by physical disability or life's harsh circumstances.

That said, self-reliance is always important, regardless of one's condition.

Today, there are horrifying situations where children and adults are kidnapped, made disabled or blind, and forced into organized begging. This has become a cruel, inhumane industry, controlled by criminal mafias.
Strict action against such exploitation is absolutely necessary.

But to identify all these nuanced situations, a donor must possess discernment and compassion — a heart that can recognize genuine need, and act with appropriate kindness or support.

As far as possible, it is better to offer food or essential items rather than giving money.
Whether you call it alms or begging, the real significance lies in the intent of the giver and the dignity of the receiver.

Here's a simple truth:
If your vessel (life) is overflowing, instead of letting that excess go to waste,
why not let it serve someone else — someone who's in need, someone hungry?

Yet, it is equally important to understand the root causes that force people into such a degraded state of begging —
uncontrolled population growth, extreme poverty, and ultimately, the collapse of moral responsibility and ethical values in society.

Until these issues are resolved, begging cannot be fully eradicated.
And therefore, what we need is not just laws, but a mature conscience, active compassion, and collective accountability. - Dhivo

--

"The eyes cannot bear to see people drowning — hence arises true compassion."

("बुडती हे जनं न देखवे डोळा - मृहणोनि कळवळा येत असे") (Budti he jan n Dekhve Dola – Mhanoni Kalwala Yet Ase" !)

One might skip visiting a temple, mosque, or church, and life would still go on…
But at least once a month, if not more, one must visit a cremation ground —
Even if it's for attending someone's funeral or final rites.

Why?
Because more than the ritualistic prayers made for personal gain,
what truly awakens the soul is the direct encounter with truth —
The truth of death, of impermanence, of what really matters in life.

Just visit a cremation ground once.
Look at a body being burned on the pyre.
Reflect on your life as you witness that moment.
And you'll see…
Your ego, selfishness, envy, pride, lust, anger, greed, attachment, delusion, arrogance — all the countless inner enemies — will collapse, fall to the ground like that lifeless body on fire.
The deeper your contemplation upon that burning corpse, the more lasting the transformation it brings to your awakened consciousness.
Let death teach you how to live. - Dhivo

--

Sweet Words… and a Throat Slit with a Strand of Hair!

(But should such beings even be called human? That in itself is a question mark.)

What happened to Saint Dnyaneshwar? Had he gone mad or something, that he chose to take Samadhi at the mere age of 21?
No, right? There must have been a profound realization.
Does a young, healthy, and highly intelligent man one day just lock himself away in a cave to enter into Samadhi? Certainly not.

He was a radiant epoch-maker walking the divine path of spirituality, a luminous soul who became a beacon of inspiration for countless brothers and sisters. After erecting the towering mountain of his immortal work, he consciously chose to enter into Sanjeevan Samadhi.

We often say spirituality is a vast and complex subject.
But epochal beings like Saint Dnyaneshwar made it simple—through their living example, their words, and their writings. They proved through their very lives that spirituality is not just a topic to discuss—it is life itself. And how life itself becomes spirituality—this has been demonstrated through the blazing work of such enlightened souls across ages.

Yet we refuse to improve.
No light seems to reach our minds.

Looking at the herd of countless seemingly civilized people like you—trapped in ignorance, claiming to be human—his heart must have ached.

"He couldn't bear to watch people drown before his eyes. Hence, the pain."
Have you ever tried to understand what Dnyaneshwar was trying to say?

He cried out: "Before my very eyes, these masses are drowning in ignorance, and I can't bear it anymore."
That is why he poured his life into awakening us—through his actions, his writings, and his timeless Bhavarth Deepika.

He didn't just try to save his own generation, but left the weapon of wisdom (Jnanāstra) in the form of the Dnyaneshwari, written in language we could understand, so future generations could also free themselves from illusion.
But we have left behind his teachings, his essence—clinging only to his idols.

Some people have even shackled the books. They worship Dnyaneshwari, Haripath, Tukaram Gatha, and Dasbodh like holy relics kept in temples, but have never attempted to understand their essence.

I say—whatever your opinion may be, at least try to understand what they actually say.
Try to practice it in life.
And if, even after doing that, you still don't like their path—then leave it. Surely, something else will suit your journey.
If you wish to follow the path of devotion, then at least first try to understand its true meaning and experience. Let there be Self-awareness, then decide for yourself.

But no—our behaviour remains like sheep following sheep.
One moves, and the rest follow blindly.

Even in temples, we go only as a formality.
Step out, and the cycle of manipulation begins again—smiling sweetly while slitting each other's throats with strands of hair.

And to justify it all, we wrap it up in excuses like:
"This is just how the world works,"
"One must deal with the world practically,"
"It's the way of the world…"

This is one of the most terrifying human dilemmas—
How can you commit such deeply deceptive acts?
One thing in the heart, another in the stomach, a third on the tongue, a fourth in the mind, and a fifth in the pocket.
Speak one thing, do another.

Where will you even hide this darkness in your heart and mind?
Cheating and manipulation have become the modern exam tricks.
Just like students hide cheat sheets—in their hair, sleeves, pen caps—
But even they would be disgusted if they witnessed this horrific act of "sweet words and a throat slit with a strand of hair."

Even Stephen Hawking, one of the top scientists of our times, has said:
“If humanity continues on its current path, we will likely destroy ourselves within the next thousand years. We must begin colonizing other planets soon.”

On the other hand, Bulgarian spiritual teacher Beinsa Douno said:
"Just as the Indian scriptures describe the end of Kaliyug and the rise of Satyug, something similar is unfolding now.
We are at the edge of Kaliyug, and the dawn of the Golden Age is beginning."

According to him, the flame of Kaliyug flickers violently before extinguishing. People are behaving in inhumane and chaotic ways.
But simultaneously, the first rays of Satyug are appearing—people’s thoughts and emotions are slowly turning toward love and truth.

Both these insights—from a scientist and a seer—are deeply profound.
But what is the actual condition of today?
And if it is wrong, how can it be changed now—by becoming aware, reflecting on the past and the future, and acting consciously today?

We need collective effort to bring real change. We must hold each other's hands and together move toward building a truly Golden Age.

Why wait for someone else to come and make it happen?
Why hope that some new messiah will appear and bring the transformation?
Meanwhile, we just keep worshipping idols like a mass mentality…

"You go fight, and we won't even hold your coat!"
Because we're too busy tearing each other down,
ripping the meat of selfishness,
and stabbing in the back with sugar-coated words.

Once, two friends were arguing—
Just like Kaliyug and Satyug locked in a debate.

I asked, "What's going on? Why are you arguing?"
One of them, Kaliyug-raj, replied sweetly:
"Hey Dada, Namaskar! When did you arrive? Come, have some water. Wait—let me make you a strong, hot cup of tea! This one here is always the same…"
I said, "Stop! Don't butter me up with sweet words just to cover the truth. First tell me what really happened."

He went silent. Truth rarely escapes such mouths. Either they sugarcoat it, or stay silent under the pretense of civility.

Then the other friend, Satyug-raj, said:
"Dada, I've been telling him not to deceive others with sweet words. Don't kick away people after using them.
But he keeps saying—'This is how the world works, everyone does it, so why should I act differently?'
He believes deceit and cunning are necessary to survive in this world.

Tell me, Dada—is that even acceptable? Shouldn't someone take the first step to change?
I told him: 'Just because someone eats dung, will you do the same?'
'If someone digs a ditch, will you call it a well?'

But this unconscious fool just doesn't understand.

He sweet-talks people while he needs them.
But once his work is done—once he knows he has nothing more to gain from someone—he starts ignoring them, opposing them, and even sabotaging them behind their back.

Those who once helped him, he now betrays.
This is the true Kaliyug form of "sweet talk and a throat slit with hair."

And he's not alone—many people act this way.

They have no real love or care in their hearts for someone, but speak to their face so sweetly you'd think the person was their future in-law!

And when they're exposed, Kaliyug-raj laughs it off.
He calls the other person crazy, trying to silence the truth.

He says, "Dada, don't listen to him. He always jokes like this. Don't take him seriously. Tell me—when did you arrive? How are things with you? If you ever need help, I'm always here for you."

Satyug-raj sighs and says,
"Dada, this is his pattern. As soon as the truth begins to leak, he discredits the one exposing it, diverts attention, and tries to hijack the narrative.

He's an expert at making false promises, offering help, and acting like a saint.
But when the moment of truth comes—he vanishes.
Just like those movie cops who arrive after the crime is over—
And then cry crocodile tears to fake their humanity."

Hearing all this, I was shocked.

How do we even begin to fix this?
How do we treat the minds and hearts of such people?

Why doesn't Dnyaneshwar's compassion enter their souls?
How have they turned to stone?

But even if a stone doesn't weep, now is the time to crack it open.

This "sweet talk and throat-slicing" may seem like a small thing—
But for the upliftment of humanity and the world, it is heavier than a mountain.

Even if not a Golden change—at least a Bronze one.
Even if not perfect—at least sincere.

Anyone who understands this, must stand tall, and act with deep conviction to transform such inhuman traits into humane ones.
Let us not wait for others.
Let each of us step forward ourselves.

Let us show true friendship, affection, and humanity.

Because as Dnyaneshwari says:

> "By persistent practice, one can illumine the heart;
Even the crippled can climb mountains with the power of effort."

Yes friends, the time has truly come—
For good people to come together.
To become better ourselves,
And guide others toward goodness.

Now is the time to plant the seeds of humanity's highest values.

Let us walk together, one step at a time,
toward the light of human dignity and compassion.
Let us breathe new life into a dying humanity. —
Dhivo (Dinesh Talekar)

--

Do not run after awards, praise, or rewards. And if someone lovingly offers you any of these, do honour them with gratitude. But beyond all this, continue to strive—relentlessly—from the core of your belly, the depth of your mind, and the innermost edge of your heart—to erect a towering mountain of your ever-evolving life's work, with your entire being committed to it… — Dhivo

--

Don't indulge in rituals just for the sake of doing something.
Even if you perform all kinds of rituals, remember this firmly — they are merely rituals unless there is depth, awareness, and purpose behind them... — Dhivo
--

World Environment Day – 5 June

"Plant Trees, Preserve Yourself!"
— Dinesh Talekar (Dhivo)

Yes, the slogan "Plant Trees, Save Trees" is already true —
but even more real is this:
"Plant Trees, and Save Yourself and Your Loved Ones!"

Each year, we're witnessing an alarming rise in heat intensity. What once felt like desert-level heat is now scorching the very soil of Maharashtra. Official temperature recordings have noted over 50.5°C in parts of Rajasthan. Even Maharashtra has crossed 47.5°C in some regions this year. Heatstroke is claiming hundreds of lives. People, animals, and even trees are perishing. But beyond them — it is water and air itself that seems to be dying.

This is not just climate change, it's climate emergency.

With a population exploding faster than a bullet train, relentless deforestation in the name of blind development, and an ever-growing obsession with comfort, luxury, and superficial "shining" — pollution has skyrocketed, pushing our environment into the ICU of Planet Earth.

Let me remind you:
When President Barack Obama visited Delhi for just two days, his doctors reportedly said he lost six hours of life — due to the air pollution in India. That is how dangerous our environment has become.

Urban India can no longer afford to pretend it’s asleep.
The explosion of pollution and depletion of water is no longer a village, city, or rural issue — it's personal. It's entering your homes, seeping into your lungs, and stealing your children’s tomorrow. You may soon need a lamp even in daylight — because the sky may forget how to shine.

While pollution levels like those in Delhi, Mumbai, or Pune might not yet have reached every village and taluka, the way things are going, that dark day is not far. But one environmental demon is already upon us — drought.

Yes, let's not beat around the bush —
Pollution and deforestation have endangered the lives of people, animals, and the environment as a whole.
And it is this very destruction that has now taken the monstrous form of drought, claiming the lives of farmers and pushing entire communities to despair.

So, what must we do?

Modern agriculture is inevitable, but not just in terms of new tech. What we truly need is innovative, affordable, and simple solutions to the real questions we face — solutions rooted in creativity and courage.

And for this, we must invoke the immortal spirit of Chhatrapati Shivaji Maharaj — not just in slogans or photos, but in real action. One of his greatest innovations was the idea of guerrilla warfare — "Ganimi Kava," or strategic intellect for survival and creation.

You see, rain doesn't fall from above on its own — it is the trees on land and the oceans that call it down. What we can control, we must act upon. We

can plant trees. We can reduce pollution. We can conserve water. And the time to start is NOW.
Let's not limit our activism to WhatsApp posts and Facebook shares about drought.
The youth must rise — with action that is scientific, humane, and future-ready.

Let's begin by gifting and planting trees — and vowing to care for them like life itself.

Together, through collective action, we can plant, protect, and nurture trees.
By doing so, we safeguard not just the environment — but ourselves, our people, and the soul of the planet.

Let's gift a sapling… Let's pledge to plant and protect a tree today!

— Dinesh Talekar (Dhivo)
Your Friend of Nature

--

"There's a vast difference between a person's mistake and a mistaken person.

If we can understand this subtle truth in human relationships,
there remains no space for misunderstandings…" - Dhivo

--

"Keep walking the path of selfless action — but a clap never resounds with just one hand, until the invisible hand of Existence —
in the form of Time —
joins in at the right place, in the right proportion..."
- Dhivo

--

Warning!
If defaming someone is a sign of mental illness, then taking interest in hearing someone's defamation could be a symptom of an even deeper mental imbalance waiting to manifest in the future... - Dhivo

--

Some people…
You never know when, where, or what will trigger them. And when it does, they don't express it then and there.
They wait — for their perfect moment —
only to spew their bitterness at you,
leaving you shocked… and speechless.
And then you're left wondering —
Should I be angry?
Or feel sorry for them? — Dhivo

--

"How to behave, and how to live?"
This remains one of the most unanswered — or at best, half-answered — and deeply profound questions of all time. : Dhivo

--

"Learn to digest everything silently" and
"Time is the greatest healer" —
A person who lives by these two sayings
can rightly be said to have boiled life and drunk it.
— Dhivo

--

It's not that such a thing can never happen,
but it is indeed rare —
that in the twilight years of your life,
you feel no regret about how you lived.

Still, there's nothing wrong in expressing regret...

But those who spend their entire lives
blaming life, others, circumstances,
or even themselves —
and keep boiling in that bitterness till the end —
it's not wrong to say that
"they never truly understood life." - Dhivo

--

Failing an academic exam doesn't mean you've failed in the exam of life.
But the one who scores less than 35% in the test of living with moral values —
in this life, he never gets another chance to reappear in that exam.

No matter how much material wealth he accumulates,
in the eyes of destiny, he still remains a failure… : Dhivo

--

I have nothing much to do with honour or insult, shame or pride, envy or rivalry...
But whether you have boiled and drunk your ego and identity, whether you have understood the dicey games of life — that is what truly matters. - Dhivo

--

"Everything is fine, everything's going great" — The moment this feeling arises, one must become more cautious, because as the day sets, the night silently begins... - Dhivo

--

In the name of rebellion,

some people are only interested in hating those they personally consider wrong,
opposing everything, and simply mocking and ridiculing others... – Dhivo

--

For peaceful sleep,
it's not just the sun that must close its eyes,
you must also shut the doors not only of your body, but of your mind… — Dhivo

--

Commando Yogi —
There's no definite answer to "How to live life?"
And even if there is, one answer can't fit all...
But try living with eyes wide open, with fierce awareness. Try becoming a Commando Yogi — if you can. — Dhivo
--

When the sun sets, darkness follows…
But even if you close not just your eyes but your mind as well, You still feel the darkness, don't you? So instead of just waiting for a way — Let's learn to carve one. — Dhivo
--

In the faint light of a lantern, you see just enough to take one step at a time — yet that's how you climb an entire mountain. The journey toward your true self often begins by groping through the darkness... — Dhivo

--

Don't be quick to judge someone's capabilities based on the early chapters of their life...
For some, the sun rises late —
but when it does, it shines with grace and glory. — Dhivo

--

"Sadhana Yoga" is truly an emotional yet scientific journey... First, live with discipline. Then, immerse yourself in meditation and focus. Then, if possible, travel towards the state of Samadhi.
If not — just move ahead with a pure and open heart on the next step of the journey... — Dhivo

--

We often wonder —

"Why can't this person do something good for themselves?"

But not all people are the same...

Some are born to be "Philosopher's Stones" (Parīs) — They turn even iron into gold, Yet remain stones themselves, wearing down silently for the sake of others… — Dhivo

--

"When the weed of misunderstanding begins to grow,
one must plough the field of the mind
with the plough of wisdom..." — Dhivo

--

"Don't hold on to hatred or anger,
don't sulk or go silent.
Never tie knots of resentment in your heart.
Learn to let go—right then and there.
Don't complicate the web of destiny any further…" — Dhivo

--

If there's even one "scientifically spiritual human being" (वैध्यात्मकि व्यक्ती) in your life,
you'll never feel a lack of light,
because scientific spirituality glows like the sun — radiant and unwavering.— Dhivo

--

A human stands right at the center of the crossroads — if only he could hear the whisper of inner distance, he could determine the direction of his journey...
Even if man cannot become Narayana (the divine), it's alright —
but let us not allow man to descend into a beast. — Dhivo

--

Some people are so cunning that even when you speak to them about humanity, love, or wisdom, they cleverly twist that very knowledge to serve their own selfish and deceitful motives... That's why atomic energy doesn't define its own destiny — it depends on whose hands it lies in: a terrorist's… or Einstein's. — Dhivo

--

Not everyone can attain the Divine through intense tapasya, meditation, or devotion —
but all are, knowingly or unknowingly, walking in that very direction...
One just needs to be careful —
not to drop a stone on their own foot along the way. — Dhivo

--

There exists a distinct mental species of people
—
When they need a favor from you,
they suddenly start staying in touch for a few days,
liking your posts on social media,
trying to impress you with random gestures.
Then, one day, they quietly ask for what they want…
And once done, they vanish —
not to be seen again for a year or more.

There's nothing particularly wrong with this,
but let's be honest — it's certainly not humane either. — Dhivo

--

"Karma-Sankhya Yogi" :

Though his way may seem ironic to some,
Compassion flows deep — from belly to heart, it does run.
"Be born, toil, die" — the world repeats this spell,
"Do it again and again" — yet he doesn't dwell.
He knows this karmic clutter expands without measure,

As some claim glory, while drowning the world's treasure.

Even if the world moves in material spin,
This path isn't of the Supreme Nature within.

He who walks the path of conscious endeavor,
A Karma Yogi — remains steady in every weather.
Though outwardly mistaken for one who indulges,
Within, he stands untouched — a Sankhya Yogi who never budges. — Dhivo

--

You don't need to eliminate the problem,
Find the resolution —
And the problem dissolves on its own...
Just as night disappears when the sun rises. — Dhivo

--

A diamond is precious, but it isn't wealthy itself — The one who possesses the diamond is.

So,
if your life holds people as rare and radiant as diamonds,
consider yourself truly rich...
— Dhivo | Dhivo™

--

"Truth" is a powerful word,
but the idea of "Justice" is even greater —
Yet, when compared to both,
it is the concept of "Right" or "Righteous"
that holds the greatest weight... — Dhivo

--

"...Up to the throat..."
What we think, what we say,
and what we actually do when life grips us by the throat —
That is where the true measure of our humanity is revealed. — Dhivo

--

"Humanness" (Manushyatva):

- By Dhivo -

It's easy to speak sweetly about "being human" from afar —
to preach kindness and compassion as surface-level talk.
But true humanity isn't proven by what we say —

it begins its trial by fire only
when life puts our own survival at stake.

Let's think to the extremes —
when pushed to the edge, our true form may be one of two:

One, like a cat.

Some starving mother cats, in the face of death,
can turn on their own kittens —
devouring them without emotion.
Perhaps that's a product of their instinct,
a law of nature sculpted over time…
But should a human being mirror such merciless instinct
when life claws at their throat?

Two, like a scorpion.

A mother scorpion gives birth knowing —
she will be consumed by her own young.
They pierce her body in hunger,
turning her into a sacrifice of flesh and love.
Yet she stands still —
silent in her divine surrender,
faithful to her dharma,
offering her body and soul
as an act of selfless karma,
attaining Nishkama Karma Siddhi Yoga,
and dissolving into the five elements —

offering herself to the Infinite Void.
Ultimately,
what we do, think, and choose
when life squeezes our throat tight
is what defines the true measure of our humanity. -
Dhivo

--

To strike not out of ego, hatred, anger, or vengeance,
but with awakened conscience and deep compassion
— as a duty born of wisdom and empathy — this is the true essence of the "Karmayogi Warrior spirit."

— Dhivo

--

A person who deeply aligns a "righteous intention"
with an "earnest action filled with longing"
is unknowingly entering the "consciousness of Karma Yoga." — Dhivo

--

People who live just to pamper their taste buds,

fill their bellies to the brim,
and accumulate wealth by abandoning morality —
they unknowingly teach us at every step
how a human being can become
his own spiritual enemy.

— Dhivo

--

It doesn't take much strength or intelligence to argue or fight...
But to truly "digest" and "understand" someone —
you must be forged in the winds, rains,
and scorching heat of life itself. — Dhivo

--

Some people spend their entire lives
exposing others' flaws, burning in jealousy,
cheating in competition without ethics, snatching and hoarding wealth,
chasing endless pleasures...
And in doing so,
they waste their rare, precious time — as rare as diamonds and rubies — only to reach death's doorstep drenched in regret, guilt, and unspoken remorse... — Dhivo

--

In life, we all need a few people who truly understand us, because we simply cannot justify ourselves to everyone we come across each day, nor can we live up to everyone's expectations... — Dhivo

--

Golden Pearls of Childhood

Part 1 – The Maternal Uncles of Shiral
Author: Dinesh Talekar (Dhivo)

Shiral is my "Mama's" village.
No, no – Shiral is my "Mamas'" village!

At first glance, there's only a tiny dot that separates the singular from the plural – but that dot means everything. And I didn't add that dot because I wasn't referring to just one "Mama" (maternal uncle). You see, I've always addressed both of my actual maternal uncles by their first names – affectionately, even intimately – as "Baban Mama" and "Bhau Mama." The same way I've always called my mother, grandmother, and aunts by their first names too.

Still, I added that dot – that plural form – because in this village of Shiral, I don't just have one or two uncles.
I have many.

In fact, this whole village is filled with my "mamas"!
Every household here feels like my own.
Because my childhood – from Grade 1 to Grade 5 – was lived in this very village.
It's my father's maternal village, my aunt's village, and most intimately, my own childhood's motherland.

If the presence of my two blood-related uncles makes me feel like a millionaire, then that tiny pluralizing dot on the word "mama" makes me feel like a billionaire. That's the richness I feel when I look back on my roots.

The list of "mamas" from my early years and the memories I hold with each of them is so vast and so deep, it could never truly end.

With Gani Mama and many of my village friends, we would dance with joy during wedding processions and village festivals. The fun we had was boundless – we'd be swept into a sky of celebration.

In the same events, the rhythm and melody that filled the air came from my other mamas – Mahendra Mama and Ravi Mama – and their musical troupe. These mamas were like the clouds of joy in my childhood skies, raining melodies upon us like a divine downpour.

Some of the village mamas even brought an open-air movie screening of "Maherchi Saadi" starring Alka Kubal and Ajinkya Deo, right in front of the village panchayat. A big white screen was tied to bamboo poles, and a large projector lit it up with magical moving images. The sound system of that time might seem ancient now, but it enchanted everyone sitting in the field, making us sway with the film's emotional beats.

On such days, my friends and I – Chintu, Bigan, Ambu, Balu, Ganu, Papu, Pashaa, Baba, Vaibho, Maruti, Inu, Ilu, Kailu, Aba – would arrive early and play around the panchayat all day, waiting eagerly for the night's show. These were our nicknames, and our playmates would gather from nearby areas too.

After dinner, families and friends would gather in the open field, sitting cross-legged under the stars, completely immersed in the joy of cinema. I can still see those scenes from Shiral playing in my mind's eye.

Another time, a movie starring Chiranjeevi called "Aaj Ka Gundaraj" was shown in front of Dhanumama's house – what a time we had!
Then there were Sarode Mama, Balu Mama from the cowshed, and many others who organized more screenings in the open grounds near the village.

During summer holidays, they even screened "Waqt Hamara Hai" by Akshay Kumar in the riverbed – imagine an "open movie theatre" inside a dry river!

Thanks to Ambu Mama and his gang, we also got to experience an "indoor film theatre" in large halls, watching movies like Mithun's Ilaka, Chandramukhi, and Suniel Shetty's Balwan. Those experiences were magic.

The list of my mamas is as long as a river: Subhash Mama, Eknath Mama, Vilas Aba, Suresh Mama, Shambhu Mama, Mahadev Bhui Mama, Vishnupant Mama, Chhatragun Mama, Balu Kaka, Dhanumama, Pandu Mama, Ambadas Mama, Munir Mama, Dattaram Mama, Saheba Mama, Lakde Mama, another Vilas Mama, Kailas Mama, Ganga Mama, Nyana Mama, Gautam Mama, Ashok Mama, another Ashok Mama, Dilip Mama, Aajbe Mama, Rode Mama, Athare Mama, Gade Mama, Panhale Mama, Sarode Mama, Kardule Mama, Jagtap Mama, Lihine Mama, Ekbote Mama, Sayyed Mama, Sheikh Mama, Madne Mama, Kamble Mama, Sambha Mama, Sundar Mama, Sanjay Mama, Duche Mama, Gaikwad Mama, Survase Mama, Jaalindar Mama, Baban Mama, Punjab Mama, Piraji Mama, Dorge Mama, Shahaji Mama, Jafar Mama, Dastagir Mama, Gulab Mama, Rohidas Mama, Giri Mama, Tupe Mama, Shelke Mama, Jadhav Mama, Uddhav

Mama, Dhuraji Mama, Parsaram Mama, Manohar Mama, Dattu Mama, Guru Mama… and many more.

Even after moving to Pune, I was blessed with "new mamas" like Aatma Mama and Ramdas Mama (Aba Mama), whose affection mirrored the love I had back in Shiral.

There were mamas from Patraa, Kanbhachi Tekdi, Shiva hills, Dhiradi, Kada, Mirajgaon, Ashti, Rui, Ruti, Hanmantgaon, Kelsangvi, Waki-Tikhi, Takli, Kanadi, Iman village – all from the five-village cluster around Shiral.
Some would give me a ride on their bicycle through the woods into the village, chatting warmly. Others, upon seeing me, would smile and ask, "Hey Dinu, how's everything going?"

Neighbors like Dhumal Sir, Basha Mama, Ekbote Kaka, Ramdas Swami, Chandrakant Bhau, Tanaji Aba, Vasant Guruji, Mukund Nana, Hari Mama, Ankush Sir, Sali Kaka, R.S. Sir, Mutkule Nana, Dattu Dada – I may not have addressed them all as "Mama," but their love was no less.

Some were more like older brothers – Yogesh Bhau, Sandeep Bhau, Sanju Bhau, Pintu Bhau, Mahesh Bhau, Raju Bhau, Ganesh Bhau, Prakash Bhau, Aslam Bhau, Kishore Bhau, Pappya Bhau, Pampya Bhau, Santosh Bhau, Anna Bhau – but their care and affection reflected the spirit of "mama."

My younger uncle, "Bhau Mama," is only a little older than me, so I ended up calling many of his friends "mama" as well.
He's dedicated, compassionate, ever-ready to help even in the middle of the night – he lives the principle "Service to others is the highest duty."
I consider myself blessed to call him my uncle.

My elder uncle wasn't very social, but he was deeply rooted in farming – a true karmayogi of the soil. He has a delightful, balanced sense of humor – a natural spring of joy that every child should experience.

Today both my mamas – Babanrao Shankarrao Aajbe and Bhausaheb Shankarrao Aajbe – remain devoted guardians of land, water, crops, and animals.

There were many mamas whose names I never even knew as a child – because when they appeared, I only knew to call them "mama." At that age, names didn't really matter.

I bow in gratitude to Existence itself for letting me remember and write even these many names and memories.

Because these names aren't just individuals – they represent an entire generation, a village, a living community.

A village is not just land or brick houses within boundaries.
A true "social village" blooms through human connection – in village squares, communal spots, temple courtyards, and evening gatherings, like a thousand-petaled lotus opening in unity.

According to science, every seven to ten years, the human body regenerates completely. Not a single cell in my body today is the same as ten years ago. My heart, brain, stomach, skin, nerves – all are new.

So the body that existed during my childhood in :Shiraal" is no longer here – yet I live on, reborn in the same body, again and again.
That's why I say – "In the childhood of my birth..."

Just as every cell contributes to building the body, every uncle, aunt, friend, teacher, and stranger helped shape the childhood of my soul.
We all go through many births within a single lifetime.

To understand the universal depth of the word "Mama," one need not look far.

Forget Duryodhana's or Krishna's maternal uncles for now.
Dive into the river of my childhood, and you will discover pearls of affection everywhere.
And the purest of all those golden pearls will bear the name – "Mama."
Because in my experience, every mama I encountered radiated sattvic (pure, virtuous) behaviour.
Their presence coloured my childhood with warmth, wisdom, and joy.

And all of this – every relationship, every interaction – was made possible by my parents: Mrs. Vijaya Diliprao Talekar and Mr. Diliprao Vitthalrao Talekar.
For that, and for the dew-drop joy of my childhood's river, I remain eternally grateful.
This childhood cannot be relived, not in this lifetime at least.
Even if I recreate the outer landscape, I cannot recreate the inner innocence, the simplicity of those experiences, the purity of those moments.

Time flows like a river, and no one can step into the same river twice – for both the river and the person have changed.

Childhood, like life itself, is a priceless, non-repeatable gift of existence – a divine garland of moments – an astonishing play between being and non-being.

There's still so much I want to write about my mamas – especially the people of "Shiraal" village. I will write more in time. But I had to begin now, before it's too late.
Because many of those mama-shaped pearls have already returned to the soil…

And during my nightly meditations, these reflections often surface.
And as I look back on life, a glimpse of Einstein's outer science and Saint Dnyaneshwar's inner science of relativity reveals itself…
And my heart overflows with gratitude.

Thank you!
To be continued...

Your nephew,
Dinesh Dilip Vijaya Talekar (Dinu) - DHIVO

--

Article: Golden Pearls of Childhood – Grandparents of Shiral
Part 2 – Remembrance of Ekbote Guruji
Writer: Dinesh Dilip Vijaya Talekar (Dinu) - DHIVO

In the second chapter of my life's story titled "Shiral" (my native village), a remarkable verse in the form of "Vasant Guruji" faded from the stage of time in his physical presence. Yet, his journey continues with the flow of time because — the "Jivatma" (individual soul), after discarding the worn-out garment of a body, continues moving forward on the path of destiny, seeking to wear a new bodily garment to evolve further.

This feeling resonates deeply in my Indian-born mind from the navel root — and finds support in Indian scriptures, literature, long-standing social philosophies, the concept of rebirth, near-death experiences, and even the latest scientific research, all of which collectively urge one to hold faith in this ancient concept of the soul's journey.

Ekbote Sir was my principal during primary school. By age and maturity, he felt like a grandfather to me. My own grandfather, Shankarrao Aajbe, shared affectionate ties with many respected figures in the village.

I was admitted to first grade in Shiral at the age of 4, while most other children were 5 or 6 years old. The first three years of my life had been spent in Mumbai, and when I came to the village, I was the son of Shri Dilip Talekar and Smt. Vijaya Talekar, who were already known and loved by the village folks. Also, I already had memorized Pasaydan, some basic numbers, alphabets in Marathi and English (barakhadi and ABCD), and Ekbote Sir, being a keen observer and a fair judge, directly admitted me to first grade.

When we moved from Vishnupant Mama's wada (house near the Gram Panchayat) to Mutkule Mama's property, we naturally came in close contact with Vasant Guruji, Bappudev Kaka, Mukund Nana, Arun Kaka, R.S. Sir, and their families. With this, affectionate bonds naturally formed with friends like Prashant, Yogesh, Sandeep, Amol, Balu, Bigan, Ambu, Papu, Ganu, Baba, Vaibhav, Maruti, Paka, Chintu, and many others from nearby homes. Due to school and neighborhood proximity, these connections grew deeper.
Today, Bappudev Kaka, R.S. Sir, and now Ekbote Guruji are no longer present in the village physically. Yet their personality ensures that the village continues to cherish their memory.

R.S. Sir had a slightly strict temperament, but whenever we met, he would always smile lightly and ask warmly, "How are you, Dinu?" I would respond with a smile, "I'm good, Sir," and he'd continue walking down the street.

Though I studied in Shiral only till 5th grade, and R.S. Sir used to teach math to higher grades, I couldn't attend his classes. But his wife, Kulkarni Madam, was a teacher in our primary school, so I naturally shared a bond with her and their children — Atul and Chhakuli — and with Sir as well. My aunt Jaymala and uncle Eknath Mama's house was also in the same area, adding to this sense of close-knit family.

People used to address Bappudev Kaka, a.k.a. Bappu Kaka or Ekbote Kaka, with just "Kaka," a term of deep respect and affection. He was a devout devotee of Lord Shiva. Every morning, he would walk to the temple, softly chanting mantras and prayers. On the way, he'd greet people with a gentle smile and hand gestures while continuing his chanting under his breath. Whenever I saw him heading to the temple, I could feel a sense of serenity in the air.

Looking back, his life exuded the discipline of "Karma Yog."
Both Kaka and Kaku were gentle, soft-spoken, and always offered blessings while speaking for the good of everyone.
We would celebrate many festivals together in front of our house, especially Diwali — which remains etched in my memory.

All our friends and elders would gather to burst firecrackers, share sweets, and greet each other.

We would live in the moment and celebrate life as one big family.

I feel forever grateful that I had the fortune to witness — with my own eyes — two distinct generations: the one wearing traditional dhotars (like my grandfather Anna and Bappudev Kaka), and the slightly newer generation wearing pyjamas (like Vasant Guruji and R.S. Sir).
I offer heartfelt tribute to the mature souls who have moved on in their journey and pray sincerely to the Supreme Soul, who dwells in the hearts of all beings, to guide them toward Sadgati (spiritual liberation).

"This is yet another golden chain from the precious pearls of my childhood memories…"
For now, I pause at this turning of memories,
Yours affectionately,
— Dhivo – Dinesh Dilip Vijaya Talekar (Talekar Daji's Dinu)

--

Whiplashes on the Flesh of Corruption…

Yes, but it's only humans who understand this — that pigs are born in the wombs of pigs and must survive by feeding on the excreta of others.

But if you asked the pigs themselves, they'd say:
"We're doing just fine!
The whole jungle is ours, wide open.
Eat as much as you want, loot all you can.
We make the rules here.
Who dares to question us?
What God? What law of karma?
What justice? What humanity?
As long as we get what we want,
as long as our greed and our luxury are fed, we don't care what's right or wrong."
And isn't that exactly the mindset
of some corrupt politicians and officers?
They keep gathering the filth of corruption
as if it were treasure
just to fill their own bellies
and spoil their own circle with indulgence.
So what exactly are you trying to say?
...And with a faint smile, I replied:
"Ah, let it be… Don't burden yourself with this.
If even you can't understand it,
how can we expect them to understand it
in this lifetime?
Even when I say,
'Through meditation I can see
the real faces behind these masks,'
...would you believe me?"

— Dhivo Social Actionist | Conscious Social Actions

--

The Boat with a Tender Sail…

When a youth —
a small boat with a tender sail,
overwhelmed with dreams and purpose —
sets out into the ocean of ambitions,
he is bound to collide
with stormy waves of despair,
failures, betrayals, humiliation,
broken dreams, deception, and exploitation.

And often,
in the eye of this cruel storm,
he's dangerously close
to being sucked into the whirlpool
called suicide.

So, whenever you see such a drifting human boat,
lost in the dark sea of life —
become their lighthouse.
Be their friend,
a silent well-wisher,
show them a new direction
with your humane courage.

And know this:

their parents will bless you with the depth of their entire soul. — Dhivo

--

How to Attain Peace of Mind?

There's a lot one can do,
but if you truly wish to do something,
then keep striving
to reach the very roots of the mind…
Because in that inward journey,
peace of mind too
begins to arrive on its own —
gently, like a natural breeze.
If we keep digging into the roots of worldly life,
our energy might just be wasted —
for worldly life seems like a tree
with no real roots…
only scattered branches
and illusory fruits and flowers
that lead us astray.
That's how it begins to feel… — Dhivo

--

Just as a tree needs
the soil to be tilled,
a seed to be sown,
and nurturing with

water and nourishment
for it to bear fruit…

In the same way,
the seed of intellect (Buddhi)
must be surrendered
into the fertile ground of righteous discernment
(Sad-Sad Viveka Buddhi)
through the conscious tilling
of life's many terrains —
with the fertilizer of deep study,
and the waters of experience.
Only then does that seed
transform into wise living. — Dhivo

--

"Some people may have nothing to do with politics, yet they never miss a chance to play cunning games —
even in close relationships." - Dhivo

--

Article: "The Limits of Humanity"

...A Whiplash of Conscience and Compassion...
Warrior Yogi Mindset : "..Boiling Blood –
..response, not a reaction..
Author: Dinesh Talekar (Dhivo)

Just as when government property is damaged, the state files a legal case against the crowd or individual responsible and recovers compensation — similarly, when someone's body is brutally attacked and severely harmed, won't the same government enforce legal action and demand heavy compensation, if not exact retaliation?

But here arises a deeper question: Whose government does the body actually belong to? Who holds the ultimate ownership of this perishable physical vessel?

The Supreme Authority, present in every atom of the universe...
The Infinite Divine Power, the One Universal Lord
—
Paramatman — the subtlest of the subtle, the grandest of the grand,
beyond time and matter, encompassing everything...

This is the lived teaching we receive through the Indian spiritual path.

> "Weapons cannot cut it, fire cannot burn it,
Water cannot wet it, and wind cannot dry it."
(Bhagavad Gita)

This soul, the Atman, is a reflection of that Supreme Divine.

It cannot be touched by any weapon.
It cannot be burned by fire, drowned by water, or dried by wind.

But the body is mortal —
It can be diseased, wounded, burned, drowned, or destroyed.
It can be damaged by weapons, reduced to ashes by fire,
or lost to the elements.

Though we may not fully comprehend what exactly leaves the body at the moment of death, we do sense that something separates, something departs.
That very something, in Indian philosophy, is called the soul (Atman).

And to walk the path of karma on this earthly plane,
the soul needs a chariot — the body.

Through this body, we perform both good and bad deeds.
But if your actions reflect cruelty and egoism at their peak,
then your ego too will be buried deep in that same soil.

You don't need Alexander or Hitler to return to remind you of this.

Slap once, slap twice — even five times —
it hurts the body and the ego.
But if six or seven brutal attackers, armed and merciless,
assault an unarmed person driven purely by their selfish motives, crab mentality, and demonic intentions,
then such a blow pierces deeper — it reaches the soul.

And if the distance between soul and God is zero kilometers,
then such an attack becomes a direct assault on God Himself.

And in such cases, the law of karma is enforced —
and the President's Rule is imposed not by the state,
but by the Supreme Judge of Fate — Destiny itself.

One must never cross the limits of humanity.
Destiny never announces its arrival.
And those who exceed their limits will eventually fall.

Be careful. Right now, you might rule the world,
but remember — Destiny is the true king.
It may arrive in any form, but fear not —
its enforcement is usually aligned with cosmic justice and law.

Unlike your ego-driven cruelty,
Destiny strikes with compassion, pain, and a sense of justice.

Book: Warrior Yogi Mindset:
Author: Dinesh Talekar (Dhivo)

--

Self-Penance Yoga Movement

Some specific individuals in our village have transformed into savage beasts… Therefore, we request all the humane-hearted villagers to grant us permission to initiate a Self-Penance Yoga Movement — so that these beasts may once again become human.

When six armed men brutally attacked an unarmed man with the intent to kill, they didn't even show the basic mercy that animals might show, let alone any human compassion. Meanwhile, their close relatives, present around them, acted like impotent spectators — they didn't try to stop the assault, but instead stood watching and relishing the barbaric scene like demons drooling over blood.

In the end, it was not locals, but compassionate travelers passing by from other towns who intervened and rescued the victim. Even then, these beast-like attackers, with metal rods, sticks, kicks, punches, inflated hoses with iron tips — continued their deadly assault on a man who had neither the strength nor the weapons to defend himself.

Even after the man collapsed unconscious on the ground, these six animals continued to strike him. And when the travelers finally tried to take the wounded man to a nearby hospital, these vultures again pounced on him. They even tried jumping off walls to break down the hospital door, cursed and threatened the doctors, saying:
"We will kill him today, no matter what."

And even now, they continue to taunt him verbally, passing loudly outside his house, playing loud vulgar music from their tractors, blaring horns, and glaring at him with animalistic hatred.

Such wicked and cowardly beasts — with brains in their knees or buttocks — deserve not words, but a beating of boots, and yet we, out of compassion, are responding only with words. One man being attacked by six or seven others with weapons?

These demonic creatures must be straightened out with the hammer of justice and humanity.

If even one or two had come at him face to face, that brave man would've taught them a lesson. He'd have made them drink bitter defeat in a fair fight.

As warriors by lineage, if we had chosen the path of violence, we wouldn't have taken long to tie them up, hang them upside down from the village gate, and smoke them with red chilies in their wounds. But we want to awaken the sleeping society by staying within the framework of the law.

Today, "humanity has been abducted" in our village. Tomorrow, in your village, humanity may be stolen. It may be strangled right before your eyes in broad daylight.

We're not strangers to Lord Ram's warrior dharma, nor to Lord Krishna's battle strategies, nor to Gautam Buddha's transformation from emperor to enlightened being. We carry the unattached spirit of surrender taught by this fertile, valorous land.

Chhatrapati Shivaji Maharaj possessed both strategy and strength, but above all, he had discerning intelligence and empathy. And we are the soldiers of Shivaji Maharaj. Therefore, we will fight within the realm of humanity.

We are devotees of Sant Tukaram and believe deeply in the path of devotion. As his followers, we walk with faith in destiny and karma, fighting for the religion of humanity.

We continue our journey guided by Dr. Babasaheb Ambedkar's principles of the Constitution. Inspired by these great souls, we will strive — from the deepest core of our navel, connected to this motherland — to keep the flame of wise humanity burning.

Therefore, we request permission to sit peacefully, with restraint and compassion, either near the village Mahadev temple or at the village gate, and carry out our Self-Penance Yoga Movement.

A few painful, thought-provoking questions:

Can you beat a fellow well-known, daily acquaintance from your own village to the brink of death?

Can six men attack one, like rabid dogs?

Can you lure someone who once lent you food to your house under the pretense of settling dues, and then set a deadly ambush with six barbaric goons?

Should a farmer's son and a farmer himself not be allowed to run a business in the village?

Does helping fellow villagers with loans mean feeding milk to a venomous snake?

Should we, as wise villagers, not question the crab-like mentality of those who only seek to pull down others — the kind of mindset that would shame even a crab, a scorpion, a snake, or a worm?

There's still so much to say…

We understand that dogs may go mad, onions may rot, milk may spoil, eggs may stink, and humans may fall sick — all naturally.
But if humans are turning into violent beasts, then we may need to conduct research and invent a vaccine, just like we did for the coronavirus.
Are we just supposed to sit and wait for that?

This heartfelt movement is a devotional offering at the feet of saints like Jnaneshwar and Tukaram, intended to bring those whose minds have turned demonic back into the fold of humanity.

We are not merely beings of flesh and bone, but mind, intellect, and spirit.
We do not aspire to become gods, but we will never become beasts, and we will keep striving to bring back those who have fallen into that state — with compassion, courage, and determination.

For now, I pause at this tender bend of self-penance.

From a humane perspective,
Please understand.

Your own village brother (Resident & student in the village: 1988 to 1996),
Dinesh Talekar – Dhivo
(Google Search: Dinesh Talekar)

"Lead me from untruth to truth…
From darkness to light."

--

To,
The Honorable Chief Minister,
The Honorable Home Minister & Deputy Chief Minister,
The Honorable Deputy Chief Minister,
The Honorable Health Minister,

Government of Maharashtra, India
C.C.:
Prime Minister's Office, Government of India
Chief Minister's Office, Deputy Chief Minister's Office 1, Deputy Chief Minister's Office 2, Home Minister's Office – Government of Maharashtra
---

Subject: Request to provide Advanced Defibrillators (AED Machine & Manual Defibrillator) at Taluka-Level Government Hospitals
---
A 9-year-old devotee of Lord Ganesha named Shivtej Sondge received an electric shock from a decorative lighting chain installed in front of a Ganpati Mandal. He collapsed instantly.

People nearby saw him, panic spread, and calls for help rang out — but these cries were drowned in the deafening sound of DJ music. Chaos broke out. Mandal volunteers rushed in. So did decorators, sound system handlers, sellers of flashy Chinese lights, donation collectors, and onlookers — all ran towards Shivtej.

The electricity was quickly shut off, the lighting chain was pushed aside, Shivtej was gently turned on his side, carefully lifted, and laid into the "well-equipped" ambulance that had been arranged by some alert political leaders for the festival. His legs were raised to restore blood flow to his heart, and CPR was immediately started. He was rushed to a "well-equipped" government hospital.

At the hospital, doctors immediately took him to the ICU, continued CPR, and used the automated external defibrillator (AED machine) available at the hospital. Despite their best efforts, the case was very critical.

But the humane-hearted doctors gave it their all, and when they used the defibrillator again on Shivtej's chest, his heartbeat resumed. Electrical shocks and pressure from the machine revived the heart's activity, and Shivtej slowly began to regain consciousness. Seeing this through the ICU glass window, his mother and father burst into tears of joy, thanking the government, administration, and hospital staff for providing such modern machines at the Taluka level.

And then, Shivtej's mother suddenly heard his voice inside her head, crying out, "Mummy-Papa, please save me!"
She woke up with a jolt from this dream, screaming "Shivtej!" in gut-wrenching agony, sobbing like a newborn calf mourning its mother. Hearing her cries, Shivtej's father came running and, lost in the memory of their son, broke down in helpless grief.

The reality:

> “9-year-old Shivtej from Ashti died due to an electric shock from the decoration lighting outside a Ganpati Mandal.”
This news headline — with Shivtej’s photo — kept flashing in front of her tear-filled eyes.

Respected Sir(s),

Yes, our 9-year-old, smiling, playful Shivtej is no longer with us.

The above narrative has been shared not as fiction, but to convey the gravity of the situation and the importance of Defibrillator machines at the Taluka level.

Had a Heart Shock Machine (either an AED or Manual Defibrillator) been available in Ashti that day, doctors could have saved Shivtej’s life.

That is the purpose of this letter — so that from now on, lives like Shivtej’s can be saved. We earnestly request that at least at every Taluka-level hospital, these machines be made available.

These machines are useful in many medical emergencies. As we all know, even young people

today are increasingly falling victim to deadly cardiac arrests.
If defibrillator machines are available, our doctors can save many precious human lives.

Please forgive us if we have overstepped, but with or without official backing, we are committed to carrying this responsibility — in memory of Shivtej.

Additionally, MLA funds, MP funds, or even public donations can be used to procure these devices. As per your directions, we are ready to follow up continuously. We will wait, we will try through every channel, and together, let us all keep humanity alive.

With a heavy heart, we thank you!

In memory of Shivtej, and as responsible, sensitive citizens:
Mr. Dinesh Talekar (Google: Dinesh Talekar)
Mr. Amrut Ajabe (FB | Insta: Amrut Ajabe)

--

To,

All Honorable and Respected Leaders of Our Village,

Subject: A heartfelt plea for justice and safety following the brutal armed attack on a villager

---

Reason for this letter:

By now, it must be known to all of you that on September 13, 2023, in our village, someone carried out a cowardly and life-threatening armed assault, akin to a gang of robbers attacking someone mercilessly…
And that is why — ("Beware of the violent and unhinged men from this household..."
— Based on the lived experience of fellow villagers)
A board with such a warning should be put up in front of their house on behalf of all villagers.

If we request this from our MLA and other senior village leaders who stand for justice,
Then such a request is not out of malice, but a legitimate step toward protecting villagers from future threats and potentially fatal attacks.

And if needed, we are ready to respectfully prove this necessity before the High Court as well.

Alternatively, those attackers could be evaluated by psychiatric professionals and declared "dangerously mentally ill," and — in a tone of bitter irony — we could even raise public donations to admit them into a psychiatric facility for dangerously violent individuals.

This might sound sarcastic, but it is actually a heartfelt plea to the compassionate and discerning conscience that lives within each of you.

And if it is proven that these perpetrators acted fully consciously, then they belong behind bars.

Such psychopathic animals — who lash out violently for the pettiest reasons or even without provocation — can attack any innocent person simply for walking alone near their home.

Should such "terrorist-minded psychopaths" be allowed to roam freely among the women, children, and the entire peace-loving society of our village and surrounding areas?

My uncle, who was attacked, is in critical condition and has been admitted to a hospital in Ahmednagar by some of his friends.
A formal complaint has also been registered at the Ashti Police Station.
He has suffered serious head and spinal injuries.
The brain and spine are made up of delicate

neurocells, forming the central nervous system — which is vital for keeping a person alive.
If this is damaged, it can cost a person their life. This doesn't need to be explained to any sensitive and sensible citizen.

We all know well which matters can be ignored, which require caution, and which ones demand uncompromised justice.

Here, my uncle — and a man who is known for always being available to help the village selflessly, even in the middle of the night — deserves justice.
We — his nephews and family — are pleading for that justice on his behalf.

The question isn't just who started it or what caused the dispute.

The real question is this:

> Is it ever justified for 6–7 men to carry out a deadly armed attack on a single unarmed villager?

We firmly state that the blame in this case lies entirely with those violent, mentally deranged individuals, and there is strong evidence to prove this — many villagers have already witnessed what happened.

We sincerely hope and trust that you, dear leaders and respected villagers, will recognize our deep concern rooted in justice and humanity, and make an honest effort to ensure justice is delivered and truth prevails.
To all the wise and compassionate villagers —
We pause here for now.
Warm regards,
Thank you! - Yours truly,
Dinesh Talekar – Dhivo

--

Beware!
Some people around you may seem good for 23 hours a day.
But the moment trouble strikes you,
in that remaining one hour,
they'll change colors like a chameleon
and won't hesitate even for a second
to pour fuel into the fire against you.
— Dhivo

--

"It's okay if, when the time came, you couldn't stand by your friend. But at least, don't be the one who adds fuel to the fire while keeping your friend in the dark.
If you failed to support your friend in need, you'll only step down from friendship.

But if you deliberately ignited the fire or poured oil on it, you'll fall from grace as a human being too." – Dhivo

--

"Caution! If there's a politician around you — at any level — or if you're within a politician's circle,
then knowingly or unknowingly, you start viewing not just your own life,
but also the events affecting society, the nation, and even the world —
through the lens of that politician's profit and loss.
That's when the term 'Political Brainwash' becomes deeply alarming and dangerously real..." – Dhivo

--

"Even if you take a true friend for granted ten times,
at the eleventh time, he might use bad words for you out of frustration —
but he won't hold grudges or misunderstand you.
Such a friendship rarely breaks.
But it's equally true — friendship is never one-sided." – Dhivo

--

Middle-Class Struggle:
"There comes a point in life after relentless struggle when it feels like the storm has settled a bit...
And just when you ease up and begin to live a little carefree,
the responsibility of that struggle returns —
forcing you to spin once again in the grinding wheel of domestic life..." - Dhivo

--

"**Sometimes it feels like certain groups** in this era of social media
might end up developing a kind of 'political cancer'.
Because during election seasons, they chew on political topics every single day
through one medium or another — in such massive amounts —
that by the time they go to bed, their brain must be on the verge of a short circuit..." – Dhivo

--

"**Whether there's a reason or not,**
this tendency is always looking for someone to blame.
It's actually a mild form of psychological disorder.

With a little observation, you'll be able to notice this pattern even around you."
- Dhivo

--

A Satirical Blow on the Habit of Criticism:

"If you're constantly criticizing someone,
gossiping behind their back,
chewing on your bitter feelings
and trying to stain their name —
and somehow that makes you feel better,
then perhaps their name should be called 'Medicine' —
because clearly, they're healing your inner sickness."

--

The True Test of Humanity:

"Even a street dog behaves well in broad daylight…
But if the night is dark and dangerous,
and you still run to help someone,
keeping your humanity alive —
then not just people, even voiceless animals will see you as a divine presence."

— Dinesh Talekar (Dhivo)

--

"We cannot claim that we'll never be insulted or never feel anger.
That's why, to respond wisely in such moments, we must strengthen our ability to digest insult and swallow anger.
In other words, we need to deepen our understanding of life itself." — Dhivo
--

Free-Time Reflection...

Sometimes it feels like certain behaviors are just a part of people's nature...
Some don't show up when it matters,
some don't value or care in time.
Some sulk over the smallest things,
while others create misunderstandings over trivial reasons.
Some, if they find even the slightest crack, go gossiping around,
some have overly sensitive ears,
and some just can't keep their mouths shut.
For some, even a little honest talk turns their nose red,
while for others, a small disagreement lifts their eyebrows.

Some start criticizing the moment you turn your back,
and some seem to be just waiting to pour fuel into any fire that starts.

And then... someone's always forwarding something…
while someone else is just sitting and reading it...
Why? - Dhivo

--

"People often say that time changes people.
But sometimes, it feels like people don't really change —
they remain exactly as they are.
It's just that during their time of need,
they hide their true face behind a mask of humility.
And once their need is fulfilled,
they remove that 'mask of need'
and freely roam around with their hidden, ungrateful face." - Dhivo

--

"Sometimes I wonder…
Am I an alien or something?
Because most of the time — actually, almost always —
no one really understands what I'm trying to say.

Then I start thinking…
could it be the same with others too?
That no one truly understands what they are trying to say either?

And then it begins to feel like…
maybe all of us have actually landed on Earth as aliens..." - Dhivo

--

"Some people who rise from poverty build their wealth through self-effort.
Among them, a few go on to create wealth for others as well.
But then, there are those who start accumulating wealth
just to show it off to others —
and perhaps it's here that their wealth may remain,
but their overall life — especially their humane and spiritual life —
begins to decline.

That's why, once you've reached the mountaintop, it's even more important to stay alert and grounded." - Dhivo

--

"Let's say, fine—leave 10% room for exceptions...
But 90% of life's situations don't require instant reaction.
And if you haven't learned even this much from your own life experiences,
then what you've lived through can't truly be called living—
Rather, as we say in village language:
'He was born... filled a few pots of water... and just passed on.'"

Reactions often emerge from the six inner enemies (Shadripus),
But responses are born from discernment and sensitivity.
That's what gives human life its authentic aliveness.

Learn to distinguish between Reaction and Response.
Not just in words or actions,
But sometimes even silence
can be the most powerful and humane response of all… - Dhivo

--

"Born with a golden spoon,
and yet—what do many privileged humans end up doing?

They spend their days pampering dogs and cats...
not even caring to raise cattle or contribute meaningfully to life.

Their priceless wealth and invaluable time
is squandered in self-indulgence and maintaining hollow prestige.

Meanwhile, sharp-eyed youth, rising from the ashes of poverty,
watch this spectacle... and learn a new proverb from you:
'This is what it means to strike the axe on your own feet.'"

--

Misunderstandings are of two kinds...
in the realm of duality.
One arises about others —
misjudging the external nature, distorted by separateness.

The other arises about oneself —
a misunderstanding of one's own inner nature.

But once you begin the inward journey
toward self-realization,
most of the external, mental-emotional illnesses — born from misunderstanding — start to dissolve.

And along with them fade
the residues of hatred and anger...”-Dhivo

--

“The true valor of Karma Yoga lies in this noble pursuit:
To transform time into action,
action into virtuous action,
and if possible,
to transform that virtuous action into
selfless action — Nishkam Karma.
Such is the highest triumph
of a conscious human effort.” — Dhivo

--

“If you don’t realize what to do
with this priceless time while it’s still with you,
then it won’t take long
for time itself to reduce your human potential to a tragic proverb—
‘Born and gone just to fetch water.’”-Dhivo

--

Sometimes, even when it's our mistake — or even when it’s not —
we feel like saying “sorry” or asking for forgiveness, just so the other person feels better and we can uphold the human duty of compassion.

But when the other person misuses that gesture to fuel the argument further,
we choose silence instead.
Not out of ego, but from the wisdom earned through our past experiences — and theirs too.
We avoid the conflict,
not because we're weak, but because we've understood that not every situation deserves a reaction. This realization often dawns while walking in a crowd
or driving through traffic… — Dhivo

--

Some people simply aren't worthy of help —
and that truth becomes clearer to us
every time we try to help them.
Yet, even after realizing this,
we shouldn't take an extreme stand.
Instead, when everyone else has stepped back,

we must help —
with emotional detachment and in proportion —
as a last resort,
not out of obligation,
but out of quiet responsibility. - Dhivo

--

Being authentic means living and behaving truly —
not just pretending or projecting that you're being real.
And the difference between the two?
It never escapes the keen gaze
of the 'Sixth Sense' —
the intuitive ostrich born
from a life that's been boiled,
sipped, and deeply understood. - Dhivo

--

Dream of Quantum Entanglement

By Dinu (Google: Dinesh Talekar – Dhivo)
25th March 2025 (Early Morning, Pune)

We were driving along the main road near Zopadi Canteen in Ahmednagar city. The vehicle took a turn toward Mandhana Bungalow Road. I was seated in the backseat, my mother in the front.

Driving us was a man dressed in simple white attire – a Gandhi cap, a kurta-pyjama. A bit of his grey sideburns was visible, with a neatly trimmed black mustache and a calm, smiling face. He was chatting with us warmly as he drove, narrating memories tied to the old neighborhood and roads.

As we reached near Mandhana Bungalow, he pointed and said:

> "That road going downward leads to your old house – Bhootkarwadi, Bhingardive Mala..."

We then turned right, continued towards Savedi, took another right, and entered a square. We stepped out. A newly built house stood right in front of us.
Mother warmly invited him,

> “Please come in for tea…”
He agreed readily. Then, looking at me, he asked:
> “You’re Dinu, right? The one they call Dinu?”
I nodded with a smile.
> “Yes.”
He replied,
> “I used to come to your house. Even when you were planning to leave for Pune, I had come then too…”
I said,
> “Your face feels familiar... but I can’t quite recall.”

We both smiled.

He said softly,
> “Come on.”

We entered the house. It was new, freshly built. In front, there was a large wall unit space on white marble flooring, meant for a TV. Wiring was visible, but the TV hadn't been installed yet.
Mother commented:
> "Sanju Dada hasn't installed the TV yet…"
He responded,
> "Can be done anytime now… the house is ready."
On one side, children were playing — one looked like little Gayatri and others. Their laughter and noise filled the space.
Mother said,

> "Let's move ahead…"

As we walked a bit further inside, voices of people chatting came from another room, mixed with the clinking of teacups and saucers — the everyday sounds of tea being served.

All three of us stood outside that room.

Mother told him,

> "That's my sister-in-law in there. Since Appa passed away, many people — from the village and elsewhere — have been coming to visit her. It's

been ten days now; she's been continuously making tea for visitors…"
He smiled again, a nostalgic, knowing smile.
We looked at him.
I was thinking hard —
> "Where have I seen him before?"

He seemed very familiar, but I just couldn't figure out who he was.

We kept looking at each other.
And then… the dream broke. I began to wake up.

As I slowly regained full awareness, it dawned on me:

It was all a dream.
But now, new thoughts began to emerge...

Questions started surfacing:

1. How were Atya (my aunt), Sanju Dada (my elder brother), and our home all part of the same house in the dream?

2. Why had that man come specifically to take us to that house?

3. Why was he describing all the familiar lanes and memories as we drove?

4. Why did mother warmly invite him for tea and talk so naturally about Sanju Dada and Atya?

5. Appa wasn't seen in the dream, but we were told people were visiting Atya after Appa's passing, and she was making tea for all of them…

6. Why did that man in white attire, with that familiar smile, feel so deeply known to me?

7. Who was that man, really, who brought us to that house?

After waking up, while pondering on all of this… suddenly, a photograph flashed in my mind.

It was a picture of Appa in his youth.

And I was stunned!

Because the man in the dream — his face, demeanor, and smile — matched Appa's young face exactly.
Same facial structure, the same thin, sharp mustache, Gandhi cap, and kurta. In the dream, he wore a pyjama, and although in the photo the lower part isn't visible, I wondered — did Appa also wear kurta-pyjama in his youth?

I had always seen him in Gandhi cap, kurta, and dhoti during his elder years.

Now my mind was surrounded by countless questions…

Why did Appa come in his youthful form in my dream?
Why was their house merged with ours in the dream?
Why did Appa come as a guide, a charioteer, leading us to that house?
In the dream, it felt like Appa had passed away in his elder form — yet was speaking to us in his younger form, walking with us, guiding us...

Almost as if he had become a charioteer — not to some other house, but to his own, which was also ours.

Maybe through this dream, Appa was saying:

> "Dinu, I used to visit you during your teenage years... later you came to see me in my elder years… but now, even though I no longer live in this aging body — you can still come home.
This house is ours.
Come home freely, lovingly.

See — I came as your guide to take you there.
In the dream, you were telling me things, showing me things, but I already knew everything…
So I just smiled silently and nodded..."

Now this could very well be my interpretation — a product of the affection and connection I feel toward Appa.
It might be different from what it actually means.

But in that dream, in that pre-dawn light, the inexplicable pull I felt toward that unknown man — the affection, the familiarity — and then the shocking recognition that it was Appa's youthful face…
That moment pierced through the layers of human connection — and left my soul wordless and teary-eyed.

In the dream (Taijasa) state, the boundaries of Time and Space are different — not governed by the laws of the physical (Vaishvanara) world.

So… should we call this a form of "Quantum Entanglement" in the Dreaming State?
— Dinesh Talekar (Dhivo)
"The people who are not present in our waking life, yet appear in our dreams to guide us home — they are always truly ours…
And dreams, though dreams in name, are in fact a living part of our reality — because they are not

bound by the logic of time, but by the mathematics of love."
— Childhood name: Dinu | Legal name: Dinesh Talekar | Spiritual name: Dhivo

--

"Sometimes, one has to swallow the bitter pill of restraint and take a few steps back — because charging ahead with boldness every single time can come at the cost of one's own life." - Dhivo

--

"Sometimes in life, there comes a moment when it's not about winning or losing, honor or insult, familiarity or unfamiliarity, right or wrong, appropriate or inappropriate. It's simply about responding — broken or whole, in whatever way possible — to that moment. Just showing up. Just being there." - Dhivo

--

— मैत्रवारी - Friends' Meet - (A Friendly Confession) —

"To be honest, I really don't have time for random timepass anymore.

But still, sometimes I come over just to see you — we talk, share secrets, wander aimlessly in silly chatter.
And even though it may seem like timepass, it's not.
You don't have to hit rock bottom or face death to understand this.
You don't need a PhD on me — even if you just passed matric,
you'd still get it: Those carefree, aimless moments we spent together... they weren't wasted time — they were life itself.
They were the purest fragments of living... lived together." — Dhivo
--

"**The only reason some bonds,** friendships, and relationships still exist today…
is because I remembered them this morning after waking up.
If tomorrow I forget —
the blame won't lie solely on my memory." — Dhivo

--

Paradoxically imagining the loss after one person's departure from this planet Earth:

When a person from our life
leaves their body and moves on to the next
journey, they never leave alone…
They silently carry with them
at least a hundred and fifty to two hundred people.
Because while they were just "our person" in our
life, in the lives of many others,
they were someone else entirely—

A grandfather, a friend, a father, an uncle, a
husband, a son, a villager, a neighbor, a relative, a
well-wisher, someone familiar and close.
And so, in a strange, almost unseen way,
this one person's departure takes away fragments
of a hundred and fifty to two hundred people—
from within those left behind.
And what remains behind,
is the silent math of absence
in the minds of all those lives
he quietly touched. – Dhivo

--

Some people appear very simple,
straightforward, and modest on the surface. They never miss a chance to showcase their so-called "virtue" or saintliness. But when the time comes, the gap between that "opportunity" and their "virtue" silently disappears… and what remains is nothing but opportunistic saintliness — a disguise

so clever, you barely even notice the shift. — Dhivo

--

After a full day of worldly struggles — job, business, responsibilities, and constant mental engagement — to remain mindful and consciously walk into sleep…
this too has become a major challenge for today's young generation. — DHIVO

--

Do seekers on the spiritual path often experience a certain "invisible confinement of memory"...? A suffocating feeling — Why can't we remember or comprehend what was before birth and after death?

— Dhivo

--

I have safely come out of many life-threatening crises — and when I look back at all those near-death moments, a deep sense arises within me that some invisible force has always protected me. We may even call it the fruit of past actions — or simply, Prarabdha Karma.

- Dhivo

--

You Have Shackled the Great Ones... O You the Shacklers...!!

By Dhivo (Dinesh Talekar)

In a vast village as big as the nation of India, a massive flood had struck the river. For thousands of years, this flood refused to subside. So, some clever and a few powerful people had prepared their own boats. But millions of common people — the majority community — were left struggling and drowning in the violent waves of this flood.

These waves, in fact, were deliberately engineered by those same clever and powerful people.
To rescue these innocent, gullible masses from the floods of ignorance and the artificial currents of customs and traditions, this Indian-sized village gave birth to a few truly great souls — the enlightened beings.

Time and again, these noble personalities would dive into the river to save the drowning people. But as they would approach the very people they came to rescue, those people — out of fear, ignorance, or foolishness — would try to shackle them instead.

They held onto their saviors so tightly that the saviors themselves began to drown.

Some painted them blue and shouted "Jai Bhim!"
Some painted them saffron and shouted "Jai Shivaji!"
And the cunning and arrogant elites? They just sat back and watched, amused from their boats.
And whenever these helpless people started improving slightly, those in the boats would casually spill a little oil onto the river again — reigniting the chaos.

Then, some egoistic, blind followers from these very drowning masses went further — they created a lake the size of Maharashtra within the river itself,
and imprisoned the great ones there.
They never allowed them to truly reach beyond the borders of the state — let alone the nation!

While hundreds of other visionaries from other countries reached global stature,
these legendary figures — who had actually risked their lives and saved people from drowning in ignorance —
were shackled with blue or saffron ropes, and confined within a lake-sized boundary.

These divine personalities, whose vision and mission were more than just global — they were cosmic,
have been tragically restricted within the grip of fake followers and self-proclaimed heirs.

To release them once again…
To let their brilliance shine universally again…
We now need another radiant, courageous, truthful warrior…

It's like this:
When someone who knows how to swim jumps into the water to save a drowning person,
and as they approach — the very person in need clings to them out of fear,
they both drown.
That's exactly what has happened with our great leaders.

They came to save us — but we wrapped them tightly in the shackles of ignorant selfishness,
branding them as either "blue" or "saffron", and reducing their universal legacy
to something as small as a state, or worse — a caste.

Aren't you ashamed?
You even celebrate multiple birth anniversaries of Shivaji Maharaj…

If you must celebrate, then do it properly — celebrate all 365 days of the year, or better yet, unite and observe one meaningful, inclusive anniversary that truly honors a global hero.

And yes — change your style of celebration. Stop the poster-flooding, sloganeering, and superficial color-fighting.

Instead, show a dignified global consciousness that befits these universal revolutionaries.

You never tried to truly understand what Dr. Ambedkar meant when he said:
"Educate, Organize, and Agitate."

Have you ever deeply pondered the spirit behind those words?

First — Educate yourself, because true awakening begins only with the right knowledge.
Then, Organize, not for egotistical power, but for justice and collective progress.
Only then should you Agitate — not for show, but as a force for transformation.

But what do you do during their anniversaries? You blast vulgar DJs, smoke, chew tobacco, drink alcohol, dance wildly, fight among yourselves — you disgrace their memory with your own chaotic ignorance.

This is not innocence.
It's deliberate selfishness.
It's a disgraceful mockery of the very ideals they stood for.

You've done the same with Phule, Shahu, Annabhau Sathe, Savarkar…
You've diluted the meaning of Dnyaneshwar, Tukaram, Swami Vivekananda, Sant Rohidas, Savta Mali, Gora Kumbhar, and Sena Nhavi.

What image are you projecting?

Just look at your posters:
On one side — a majestic image of a saint or warrior in a dignified outfit with powerful eyes…
and on the other side — you, in flashy kurtas, collars up, sunglasses on, phone to ear, gold chains swinging...

What are you even trying to prove?
Your foolishness?
Or that you've deliberately conspired to defame these great souls?

Is this how you repay them?

Now ask yourself honestly —
Has your brain really been chemically damaged?
Have your nerves gone senseless?

Has someone corrupted your very DNA and semen?

Stop using the great leaders for your selfish gains. Do not imprison their humanistic legacy in the tiny cage of caste and politics.

Let their contributions and personalities flow freely — across the globe, across time.
Rise. Awaken!
Educate, Organize and Struggle —
For the creation of a luminous Swarajya,
For a disciplined freedom,
For an inclusive, holistic development of all. — Dhivo
--

"Dear Friend, Pay Attention to Life — Leave Alcohol, Sweeten Your Own Life!"

If you really want to drink,
then boil life and sip it.

Why do you keep finding petty reasons to drink alcohol, my friend?
Quit it today — not just a peg, not even a single drop.

Today, hold life's hand again — anew.

Live not only for others,
but also for yourself.
Live freely…
like a flowing river,
like a free-blowing wind,
like the rustling trees touching the sky
with chirping birds singing beside you.

Live, yes live —
but stay awake while living, my friend.

Someone planted this illusion that
"to live unconscious is to truly live."
Break that illusion — and then live.

If you must drink,
then pour a little pain into hot water,
add your own anger, greed, jealousy, ego,
and any other inner toxins — then drink that
bravely.
Swallow misunderstandings and despair —
sometimes in hot water,
sometimes cool it down with ice,
and gulp it down with your nose pinched shut.

But from today,
don't touch alcohol again —
don't fall into the trap of any "dark flocks."

Don't hand over the control of your mind,
your brain, your senses — to anyone else.

From now on — no more alcohol.
If I've said something wrong, forgive me.
But make this decision final:
ALCOHOL — CLOSED. STOP. — Dhivo

--

Krishna-like Friend:

How many people in your close circle are truly like this —
those who, at the right moment,
dare to speak the bitter truth to you,
even if it stings your ego,
even if it goes against you —
because you really needed someone to pierce your ears with truth at that time?

That, right there, tells you —
how many real people you've earned in life,
and how much life you've truly boiled and drunk.

If, throughout your life, the only people who always speak sweetly to you are your mother and your children,
then that's natural —
because both (or either one of them)
eventually move on:
Your mother may leave in physical form,

and your children, once grown,
fly off like birds from the nest.
Then, no one remains to speak sweetly to you.
Still, even their memories may be enough to guide you through the rest of life.

But… a father figure, an elder brother, or a Krishna-like friend — these are rare blessings.
It takes fortune to find someone like that —
someone who, with their bitter yet loving words, dares to correct you at the right time. — Dinesh Talekar (Dhivo)

--

When You Slow Down Life's Pace...

When we slow down the rush of living and truly observe, we begin to realize —
how abundantly rich we are, and how deeply we should feel grateful for this life.

It's when life is dragging us forward at full speed — even if we can't or don't have the time —
that we must still choose to pause...
to stop for a while and live a little.

Because once life forces you to stop,
you won't be able to run anymore —

and worse, you may find no way out either, my friends...

Who really understands life anyway?
But if along this uncertain journey,
you are blessed with — a healthy body, a pure mind, loving souls, and a wise, embracing nature by your side...

Then maybe, just maybe, you should bow to life, wash its feet, and drink that sacred water with reverence...
Don't you think? — Dhivo

--

This isn't just about alcohol, my friend…
It's about awareness.

I'm saying this out of genuine concern —
This is not merely about drinking... It's about being awake inside. Because honestly, do we really need alcohol to lose ourselves?
Aren't we already so numb —
so unaware of what's happening around us? Then what difference does alcohol or addiction really make?

Let me say this more ironically, listen...
Even if your idea of friendship is just

having fun, partying, drinking, feasting —
still, a real friend, someone who genuinely gives and receives from the heart — can dive into not just a swimming pool, but a whole ocean to pull his friend out safely… even if he's drunk.

What matters is — the heart inside must be awake. There must be care for others. When that awareness and compassion live within, then even a party with alcohol stays within bounds. But the truth is — losing consciousness doesn't come only from alcohol…
There's a far more dangerous unconsciousness that numbs our humanity, and that's what we really need to wake up from. — Dhivo

--

Wife is a blessing — realise her worth before it's too late.

Some husbands fail to recognize the value of their own Griha Lakshmi (Goddess Laxmi of the Home) — their wife — even while she's right there beside them. They forget that her parents offered a piece of their heart, tied to the knot of marriage… That she was lovingly sent from the sacred courtyard of her home,
like a Tulsi plant (Basil) offered with reverence, into a new household — yours.

But sadly, some men only understand her value
when time turns against them,
or worse — when she's no longer around.

It's true — if you can't see her worth now,
she may seem as ordinary to you as "ghar ki murgi daal barabar" (familiarity breeds neglect).
But fate flips its coin at the most critical hour,
often leaving regret in its wake.
So don't wait.
Give your wife your time, your love, and the respect she deserves — not someday, but today, and always. — Dhivo

--

"A person who speaks clearly and directly"
may seem sharp or bitter to the tongue of the mind,
but in truth, such a person helps shape your life —
bringing alignment to both your mind and your actions.

And "a person who listens with clarity"
is someone who genuinely tries to understand the other.
Such a listener protects themselves from misunderstandings,
and also makes sincere efforts to ensure others aren't misunderstood either.

— Dinesh Dilip Talekar (Dhivo)
Facebook.com/DineshTalekarDhivo

--

Dhivo Yoga Meditation Spirituality Center
Dhivo.in | Dhivo.org | DhivoYoga@gmail.com

Meditative Yoga International Organization
Facebook.com/MeditativeYoga

Social Actionist Organization
Google Search: Social Actionist
--

Together we can try to make this world more Creative, Compassionate & Conscious with more Love, Laughter & Longevity towards more Health, Happiness & Harmony.. - Dhivo

www.ingramcontent.com/pod-product-compliance
Ingram Content Group UK Ltd.
Pitfield, Milton Keynes, MK11 3LW, UK
UKHW021407190726
13845UKWH00028B/940

9 789334 361506